W9-CEJ-594

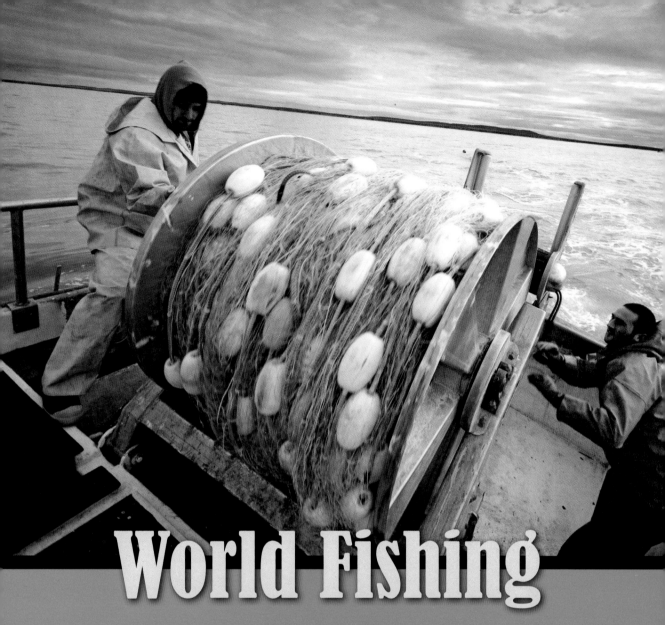

# World Fishing

## Jonathan Bocknek and Charles Piddock

MEDIA ENHANCED BOOKS
AV²
BY WEIGL™
ADDED VALUE • AUDIO VISUAL

www.av2books.com

AV² provides enriched content that supplements and complements this book. Weigl's AV² books strive to create inspired learning and engage young minds in a total learning experience.

## Your AV² Media Enhanced books come alive with...

 **Audio**
Listen to sections of the book read aloud.

 **Key Words**
Study vocabulary, and complete a matching word activity.

 **Video**
Watch informative video clips.

 **Quizzes**
Test your knowledge.

 **Embedded Weblinks**
Gain additional information for research.

 **Slide Show**
View images and captions, and prepare a presentation.

 **Try This!**
Complete activities and hands-on experiments.

**... and much, much more!**

Go to **www.av2books.com**, and enter this book's unique code.

**BOOK CODE**

**K393883**

**AV² by Weigl** brings you media enhanced books that support active learning.

Download the AV² catalog at **www.av2books.com/catalog**

**AV² Online Navigation on page 48**

Published by AV² by Weigl
350 5th Avenue, 59th Floor
New York, NY 10118

Websites: www.av2books.com   www.weigl.com

Library of Congress Control Number: 2014940095

ISBN 978-1-4896-1114-7 (hardcover)
ISBN 978-1-4896-1115-4 (softcover)
ISBN 978-1-4896-1116-1 (single-user eBook)
ISBN 978-1-4896-1117-8 (multi-user eBook)

Printed in the United States of America in North Mankato, Minnesota
1 2 3 4 5 6 7 8 9 0  18 17 16 15 14

052014
WEP090514

Weigl acknowledges Getty Images as its primary image supplier for this title.

Every reasonable effort has been made to trace ownership and to obtain permission to reprint copyright material. The publishers would be pleased to have any errors or omissions brought to their attention so that they may be corrected in subsequent printings.

Project Coordinator: Aaron Carr
Art Director: Terry Paulhus

# World Fishing

# CONTENTS

AV² Book Code ........................................ 2

Introduction to World Fishing ............. 4

The Growth of Fishing ......................... 6

Issues Facing the Fishing Industry ..... 14

Mapping the World's Fishing Areas .... 20

Threats to Marine Resources .............. 24

The Future of Fishing ......................... 32

Fishing through History ..................... 36

Fishing Careers ................................. 38

Key Fishing Organizations ................... 40

Research a Fishing Issue ....................... 42

Test Your Knowledge ........................... 44

Key Words ....................................... 46

Index ........................................... 47

Log on to www.av2books.com ..................... 48

# Introduction to World Fishing

Fishing today is a huge industry. Day and night, fleets of fishing boats search the oceans to bring in thousands of tons (tonnes) of fish and other marine, or sea, animals. Fish are an essential food source for humans. The world catch of fish also provides **fishmeal** to feed farm animals. Today, the fishing industry faces several challenges, such as declining fish populations and threats to the health of the oceans. Answers may include breeding new kinds of fish and dealing with changes in Earth's climate.

## The Growth of Fishing

"Huge fishing boats called factory ships or fish processing vessels use many kinds of nets and technology to bring in vast quantities of fish."

## Issues Facing the Fishing Industry

"The fishing industry is now a global business. Around the world, people harvest fish, consume seafood, and reduce international fish supplies."

## Threats to Marine Resources

## The Future of Fishing

"Today's marine resources are at risk in many ways. Most of the threats come from humans and their way of life."

"The future of world fishing may lie in farming and harvesting fish in new ways."

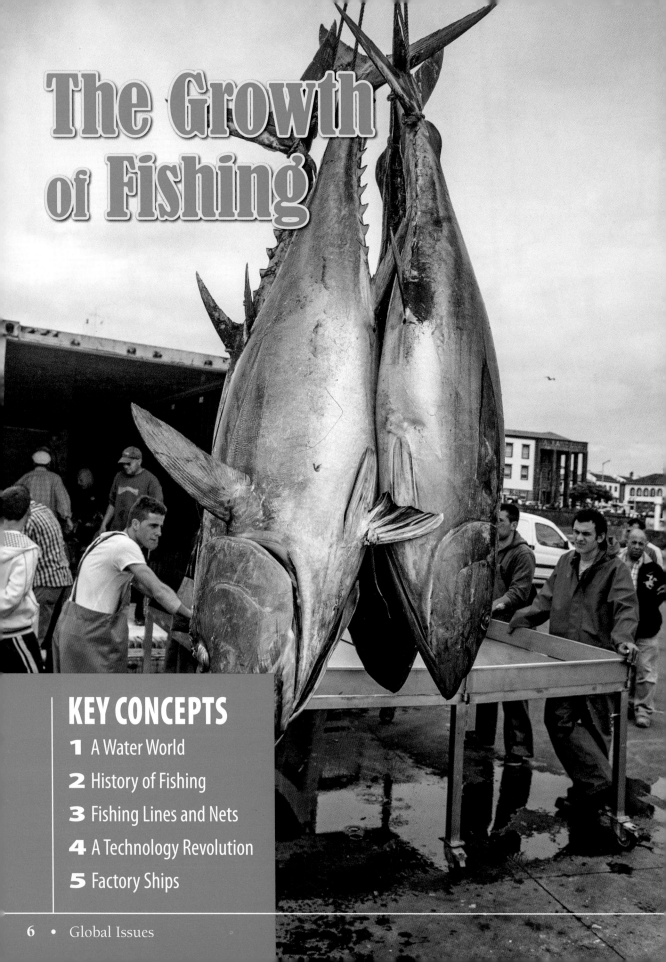

# The Growth of Fishing

## KEY CONCEPTS

**1** A Water World

**2** History of Fishing

**3** Fishing Lines and Nets

**4** A Technology Revolution

**5** Factory Ships

**T**he world's oceans have fed the human population. They have also helped people around the world earn their livings. Over the years, fishers have made many changes in the ways that they search for and capture fish.

## 1 A Water World

Earth is often called a "water world." That is because water covers about 70 percent of its surface. Most of this water is made up of oceans and seas.

Throughout Earth's history, many **organisms** have lived in the oceans. Scientists estimate that today there are more than 2 million different **species** of marine life. They range in size from tiny, single-celled organisms to the 120-ton (109-tonne) blue whale. There are more than 15,000 fish species. Humans commonly eat only about 30 of them.

All ocean life is part of an ecosystem. An ecosystem is a network formed by the interaction of plants and animals with the environment. For example, the ocean ecosystem is based on tiny, free-floating organisms called phytoplankton. Phytoplankton convert the energy of sunlight into food that is rich in stored energy. This occurs through **photosynthesis**. Small marine animals eat some of the phytoplankton. These animals then provide food for larger fish, such as cod and tuna. Cod and tuna, in turn, provide seafood for humans to eat.

This is part of a system of connected food chains called a food web.

The number and variety of species in a region or an environment, such as an ocean, is called biodiversity. Biodiversity in the oceans benefits humans. In addition to being a food supply, ocean organisms provide materials that are used in medicine and industry.

### Earth's Water Resources

Almost all of Earth's water is salt water, found in the oceans. Less than 3 percent is drinkable fresh water. Most fresh water is frozen in large ice masses in the Arctic and Antarctic. Less than 1 percent of Earth's water is usable by humans. This water is either in lakes and rivers or **groundwater**.

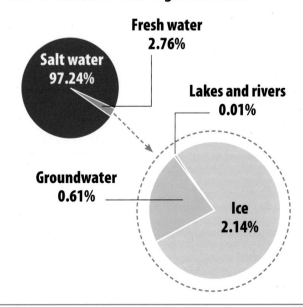

Fresh water
2.76%

Salt water
97.24%

Lakes and rivers
0.01%

Groundwater
0.61%

Ice
2.14%

# 2 History of Fishing

Fishing is an ancient practice. It dates back at least 40,000 years. Shells, fish bones, and cave paintings from long ago show seafood was part of the human diet. The very first permanent settlements almost always depended on fishing.

Early peoples probably used spears to catch fish and other sea animals. As civilization developed, people learned more effective ways to catch seafood. Fishers in ancient Egypt used hooks and nets, as well as **harpoons**. They fished from simple boats made of reeds and developed metal **barbs** to help catch fish. The ancient Nile River was full of fish, and dried fish was a staple food for much of the population. The Egyptians and other ancient peoples made different types of nets to catch specific fish.

In 110 BC, the Romans gathered oysters living in the water. Roman artwork shows people fishing from boats with a rod and line, as well as using nets and traps. Traps are nets designed to catch fish and prevent them from escaping. Almost every dish eaten in Roman times contained a special fish sauce called garum.

Fishing was also widespread in ancient Central and South America. In North America, native fishers used canoes made from trees such as cedars. They made natural fiber nets from the inner bark of trees.

The ancient Greeks caught cod using nets thrown from boats.

# 3 Fishing Lines and Nets

Today, fishers still use hooks, lines, nets, and traps for large catches of fish. One large-scale way of fishing is called longlining. In longline fishing, vessels string and drop a line with as many as 30,000 baited hooks.

Drift nets hang down in the water without being anchored at the bottom. They drift with the current of the water. Fish swim into the net and are caught. The size of the fish that are trapped depends on the size of the mesh. The first rope drift nets were made of **biodegradable** material. Today's drift nets are made of synthetic products, so that they will last longer.

Purse nets are huge nets that look like a bag with a drawstring top. The net surrounds and then closes on **schools** of fish. Once the fish are caught, fishers tighten the lines and pull the entire net aboard their vessel. Purse nets can measure more than 0.5 miles (0.8 kilometers) wide, with a depth of more than 492 feet (150 meters).

Trawl nets are baglike nets pulled by fishing boats through the water. The boats that use these nets are called trawlers. Mid-water trawlers pull the nets through the water. Bottom-trawlers use weighted, cone-shaped nets that end in a tightly meshed bag. Large boards hold open the wings of these nets, which drag across the seafloor. Powerful machines are used to pull the heavy load of fish and other sea animals aboard the ship.

A purse net is often used for capturing fish species that swim in schools close to the surface, such as sardines, mackerel, anchovies, and herring.

# 4 A Technology Revolution

Advances in all kinds of technology have greatly transformed **commercial** fishing. Before the 1970s, fishing far from shore was considered unprofitable. Fish in deep waters were difficult to find. Today, modern fishing boats contain electronic equipment that pinpoints the location of fish swimming at great depths. From high above Earth's surface, satellites use special sensors to determine the location of schools of fish under the sea's surface. The satellites can also help fishers identify the **target fish** and avoid other creatures.

Fishing boats, too, have changed a great deal. The development of **distant-water ships** with comfortable living spaces and up-to-date communication systems has improved the lives of many fishers. Requirements such as more training and better equipment have also improved safety in this traditionally dangerous industry.

During much of the 20th century, **traditional fisheries** in Europe and North America declined steadily. Local fishers were unable to compete with modern ships. The decline of small-scale fisheries left large numbers of people unemployed. Even so, traditional fisheries, mainly in **developing countries**, continue to provide much of the fish consumed by humans around the world.

Electronic fish finders help determine how deep a school of fish is swimming. Using this kind of technology can mean the difference between a catch's success or failure.

# Should Countries Pass Laws Protecting Traditional Fisheries?

**M**odern commercial fishing has grown rapidly. It has forced a number of traditional fisheries in North America and Europe out of business. Families that have fished the sea for centuries struggle to survive.

### Fisher Families

Fishing is our way of life, as it was the way of life of our ancestors. We deserve to be able to make a living at it. The government must pass laws protecting our fishing grounds from the huge fishing ships.

### Government Fishing Officials

Traditional fishing communities are an important part of our history. We must support them however we can. However, these populations are declining, and they do not have the influence they once had with politicians.

### Economists

Modern efficient fishing fleets are able to catch more fish than traditional fishers. They also provide fish at lower cost to consumers. However, traditional fishers need help to prepare them for jobs in other fields.

### Fishing Fleet Owners

In past times, fishing at sea was a difficult demanding job. Modern fishing fleets are now able to do the job of fishing more productively, more safely, and with less harm to the environment. We represent a vast improvement.

| For | Supportive | Undecided | Unsupportive | Against |

# 5 Factory Ships

Today, huge fishing boats called factory ships or fish-processing vessels capture vast quantities of fish. Depending on the type of factory ship, the fish may be cut apart, frozen, and processed on the boat. Some vessels catch and process fish into ready-to-sell fillets within hours. Onboard fishmeal plants process the waste products into animal feed. Factory ships rarely dock. They remain afloat 24 hours a day while smaller ships ferry the frozen catch to shore.

Currently, the world's largest factory ship is the $100 million *Lafayette*. This 700-foot (213-m) long ship processes more than 1,500 tons (1,361 tonnes) of fish a day. Five super-trawlers and seven fish-catcher boats pull alongside the *Lafayette* and pump their catch into one of its 32 refrigerated holding tanks. From there, the fish are sucked by vacuum to conveyer belts. Then, they are graded for size and freshness. Crew members sort 15 tons (13.6 tonnes) of fish every hour.

In some parts of the world, this kind of fishing has led to sharp declines in fish populations. Fishers who use traditional methods have found their catches reduced. Recently, species in some heavily fished areas, such as jack mackerel in the southern Pacific Ocean, have declined by more than 60 percent in a period of just a few years.

Factory ships are designed to remain at sea for months at a time. They return to port to get supplies and refuel.

# Should the Use of Gill Nets Be Allowed?

Gill nets hang straight down in the water, like curtains. They may be hung from ships or floating **buoys**. They catch fish by the **gills**. Weights on the bottom hold the nets in place. Fishers take huge catches of target fish, as well as many other unwanted marine animals. Dolphins, small whales, and turtles often get caught and die in gill nets. Since 1991, gill nets have been prohibited in international waters. However, they are permitted in coastal areas.

**Fishers**
Fishers cannot be blamed for using the most effective hunting methods. Without effective nets, we cannot catch the amount of fish needed to stay in business. Large gill nets help us survive.

**Fishery Officials**
The sea has abundant animal life, and many creatures get caught in nets. This is an unfortunate situation. However, fishers using gill nets provide large quantities of food for the world's growing population.

**Marine Ecologists**
Modern gill nets unintentionally hurt or kill sea life. They may permanently harm the health of the world's oceans. Fisheries must look for safer ways to catch fish.

**Animal Rights Defenders**
The killing of marine life, especially dolphins, turtles, and whales, through the use of gill nets should stop immediately. Gill nets are killing our ocean world and should be completely banned.

 For          Supportive          Undecided          Unsupportive          Against

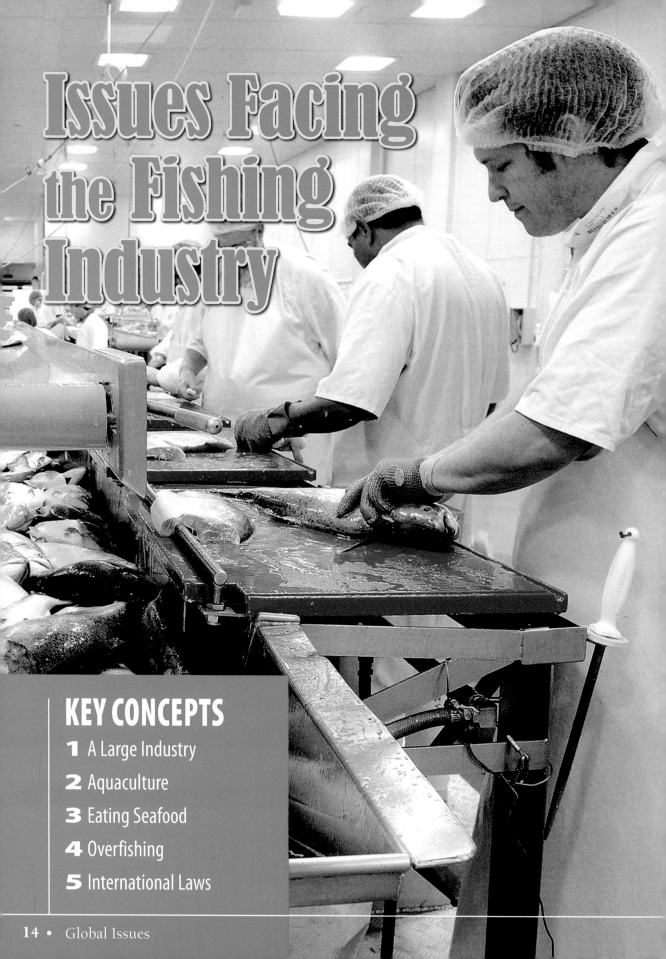

# Issues Facing the Fishing Industry

## KEY CONCEPTS

**1** A Large Industry

**2** Aquaculture

**3** Eating Seafood

**4** Overfishing

**5** International Laws

T hroughout much of human history, people fished and ate their seafood locally. Unless preserved by salt, fish tended to spoil quickly. Buying, selling, and transporting fish between countries and regions was minimal. Modern technology makes it possible to prevent spoilage and ship fish long distances. The fishing industry is now a global business.

## 1 A Large Industry

Today's fishing industry is a worldwide multibillion-dollar operation. It employs millions of people in many nations. In 2011, the global catch from the sea was 90.9 million tons (82 million tonnes). The same year, the U.S. fishing industry had $129 billion in sales. It provided 1.2 million jobs, including fishers, seafood processors, and **retailers**.

The fishing industry provides seafood, rich in **protein**, for the world's population. Today, one billion people, mainly in the developing world, rely on fish as their primary source of protein. Commercial fishers harvest a wide variety of animals, from tuna and other fish to clams, crabs, squid, and scallops.

Global consumption of fish has doubled in the past 30 years. Both population growth and rising incomes, especially in Asia, have led to increased seafood sales. Rapid economic growth in China has been a major factor. Cod caught in the north Atlantic Ocean appears on the menu in restaurants in China. At the same time, shrimp from waters near Southeast Asia are for sale at fish markets in Paris, France.

The largest markets for seafood products today are the United States, Japan, and the European Union.

## 2 Aquaculture

Aquaculture, or fish farming, has grown rapidly and is overtaking traditional fisheries in global production. Fish farmers now raise fish from eggs in a pond, tank, or contained area of the sea. They feed, track the growth of, and harvest the fish.

Aquaculture has grown from 5 percent of total world fish production in 1970 to nearly 50 percent in 2013. Nearly two-thirds of global aquaculture takes place in China. Farmed salmon now make up about half of global salmon production. Shrimp farming contributes about one-fifth of global shrimp output. Oysters have long been cultivated in farmed offshore beds. Farming of other shellfish, such as mussels and clams, has increased rapidly since the 1980s.

However, fish farming has its disadvantages. Aquaculture results in a buildup of waste matter in the water. It discharges substances that contribute to the growth of **algal blooms**. It requires large amounts of fishmeal to feed the farmed fish. Single-species farmed fish also can be vulnerable to diseases.

## Aquaculture Production of Food Fish by Continent

The term *food fish* includes aquatic animals such as fish, **crustaceans**, **mollusks**, and sea urchins. In 2012, the world's total aquaculture production was 73.4 million tons (66.6 million tonnes).

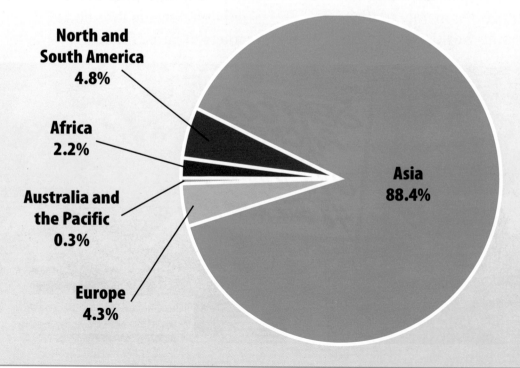

North and South America 4.8%

Africa 2.2%

Australia and the Pacific 0.3%

Europe 4.3%

Asia 88.4%

# Should People Work to Protect Tuna Populations?

Today, growing markets for tuna have pushed prices to high levels. A single adult tuna is worth many thousands of dollars. Increased catches of this valuable fish have led to the near **extinction** of some types of tuna. A 2011 U.S. government report declared that five tuna species were at risk of becoming **endangered**. Southern bluefin tuna were already endangered.

**Environmentalists**
The loss of even one species of tuna weakens the entire ocean **biosphere**. The consequences could be severe.

**Supermarket Shoppers**
Of course, people should support the protection of the sea's tuna populations. However, I still want to continue to eat safe, delicious tuna.

**Economists**
A growing market for high-quality tuna will make it hard to control the loss of some tuna species. As long as there is demand for fresh tuna, fishers will continue to catch it.

**Tuna Fishers**
It is very difficult for fishers to refuse the opportunity to catch a high price for a single fish. We love to make a living. Tuna fishing brings in the income my need to feed my family.

For          Supportive          Undecided          Unsupportive          Against

## 3 Eating Seafood

For many people in the United States and other **developed countries**, seafood is an appealing food choice. Fish is rich in many vitamins and minerals, as well as protein. It is a low-calorie food that is also low in saturated fat. Saturated fat is found in high amounts in meat, and it may raise a person's risk for heart disease.

Fish contains omega-3 fatty acids, which are required for healthy human development. Some research has shown that omega-3 fatty acids in ocean fish helps protect against heart disease and improve brain function. Studies highlight low rates of heart disease among groups who tend to eat a great deal of fish, such as the Japanese and Inuit peoples.

"People around the world have never eaten more fish. Today's annual fish consumption is at an all-time high of almost 37 pounds (17 kilograms) per person."

Fish is an especially important source of protein in developing countries. In more than 30 countries, fish accounts for at least 50 percent of protein consumed. These countries include Bangladesh, Ghana, and Indonesia.

People around the world have never eaten more fish. Today's annual fish consumption is at an all-time high of almost 37 pounds (17 kg) per person. Experts at the Food and Agriculture Organization (FAO) of the United Nations (UN) say another 40 million tons (36 million tonnes) of seafood will be required worldwide per year by 2030 to keep up with population growth. Also, as the number of cattle, hogs, and chickens grows, so does the demand for fishmeal to feed them.

Raw seafood prepared with rice is called sushi. People around the world eat this Japanese dish.

# 4 Overfishing

Each year, fishing fleets travel the seas searching for larger amounts of seafood to feed the world. The result has been overfishing in many places. Overfishing occurs when the number of fish harvested is greater than the ability of fish to reproduce. Fish populations become smaller, and some species face the risk of dying out in certain regions. This is a threat to the species and the ecosystem, as well as the fishing industry.

Other species in the marine food web suffer when a fish **stock** is greatly reduced. For example, growing numbers of starving seals and seabirds, as well as undersized fish and whales, have been linked to declining populations of the species these animals depend on for food. Overfishing of herring and capelin in the Barents Sea off the coasts of Russia and Norway led to a sharp drop in the Arctic cod population. In the northwest Pacific Ocean, sea lions numbered about 300,000 in 1960. Today, the population has dwindled to 40,000. The likely cause is intensive fishing of the sea lion's most important food source, Alaska pollock.

Setting quotas, or limits, on fish catches is one answer. There are a growing number of agreements among nations, as well as rulings by international organizations, to protect the oceans, their ecosystems, and their fish stocks. However, progress has been slow.

## Status of Global Fish Stocks

In 2010, 75 percent of the world's fish species were fully exploited, overexploited, or depleted. Fully exploited means that a fish stock is harvested at rates near its ability to be **sustainable**. Overexploited means a fish stock is being harvested at rates that are not sustainable in the long term. Stocks become depleted. When a fish stock is depleted, catches are well below historical levels, no matter how much effort is spent.

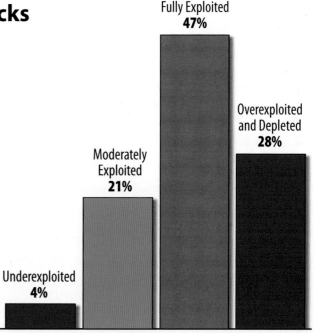

# Mapping the World's Fishing Areas

**1**

**14**

**2**

Pacific Ocean

North America

**16**

The FAO separates the oceans into 19 fishing areas. The fishing areas in the Pacific Ocean account for almost 47 percent of the world's total catch of ocean fish.

**4**

Atlantic Ocean

**5**

**18**

South America

**17**

**7**

## Legend

**1.** Arctic Sea
**2.** Northwest Atlantic
**3.** Northeast Atlantic
**4.** Western Central Atlantic
**5.** Eastern Central Atlantic
**6.** Mediterranean and Black Sea
**7.** Southwest Atlantic
**8.** Southeast Atlantic
**9.** Atlantic (Antarctic)
**10.** Western Indian Ocean
**11.** Eastern Indian Ocean
**12.** Indian Ocean (Antarctic)
**13.** Northwest Pacific
**14.** Northeast Pacific
**15.** Western Central Pacific
**16.** Eastern Central Pacific
**17.** Southwest Pacific
**18.** Southeast Pacific
**19.** Pacific (Antarctic)

**19**

Arctic Ocean

1

3

Europe

Asia

6

Africa

13

Pacific Ocean

15

Indian
Ocean

10

Australia

11

8

N

W    E

S

17

12

9

SCALE                    1,200 Miles

1,200 Kilometers

19

# 5 International Laws

Until the 1970s, most of the world's oceans and seas were considered international waters. They were open to fishers from all nations. In 1972, Iceland became the first country to claim an extended fishing zone of 50 nautical miles (90 km) from its coasts. This area was barred to fishing ships from other countries. Iceland increased this area to 200 nautical miles (370 km) in 1975.

In time, other countries followed. In 1982, the UN Convention on the Law of the Sea (UNCLOS) established exclusive economic zones. A country could bar others from fishing in an area up to 200 nautical miles (370 km) from its official coastlines.

The governments of many countries have passed regulations to safeguard their national fishing grounds. These regulations cover everything from quotas on catches to types of fishing gear that can be used. However, the value of fish on the world market has risen so high that some fish populations are becoming dangerously low. Many fishing boats ignore the zones, take fish, and return to international waters without penalty because the rules are hard to enforce.

Most major fishing nations are cooperating to protect their fishing resources. For example, Iceland and the United States currently use a strategy of fishing quotas and strict enforcement of conservation measures to protect marine resources. This has enabled large-scale fishing to take place without depleting fish stocks.

The U.S. Coast Guard has more than 42,000 active duty personnel to protect and maintain U.S. coasts and fisheries.

47209　U.S. COAST GUARD

# Should Governments Enforce Fishing Zones More Strictly?

The UNCLOS agreement outlines the rights and responsibilities of nations in their use of the world's ocean. It also sets up guidelines for countries to use for regulating industries, protecting the environment, and managing ocean resources. Enforcement is mostly the task of each government.

**U.S. Fishers**
Stricter enforcement of these regulations in U.S. waters would ensure bigger catches for us. It would also strengthen protection of fish species. Our laws must be enforced.

**UN Officials**
We encourage governments to follow the international law. It benefits all national fisheries. However, individual countries are responsible for their own rules within their zones.

**U.S. Coast Guard Officers**
We try to enforce these laws, but the task is challenging. We do the best we can with our aircraft and ships, but it is a huge job.

**U.S. Government Officials**
To oversee our zone more strictly requires much more money than we have. There is also the issue of maintaining positive relationships with other countries. Sometimes, that may be more important than supporting U.S. fisheries.

For     Supportive     Undecided     Unsupportive     Against

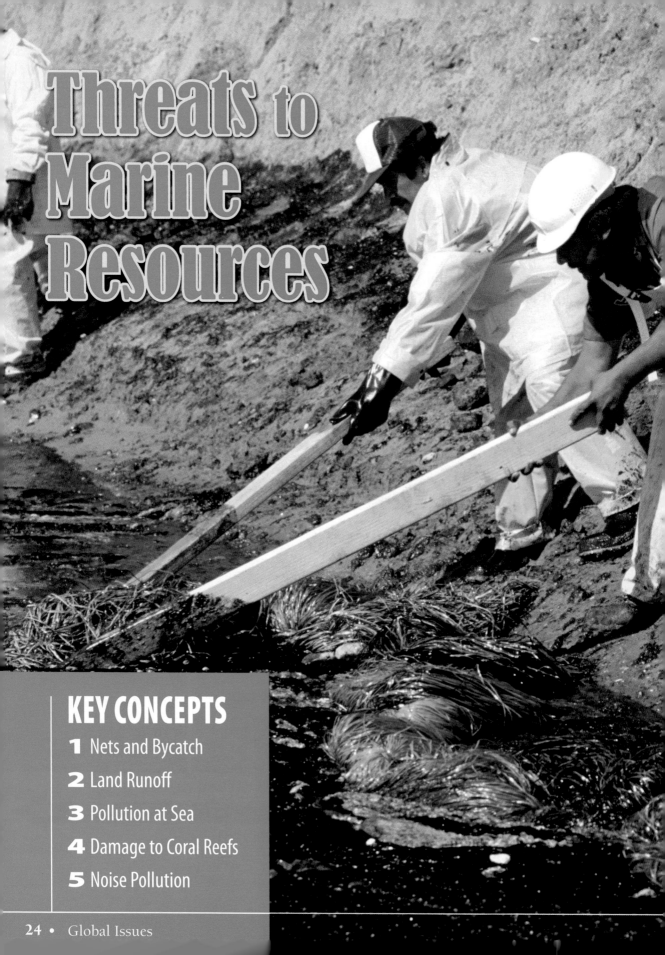

# Threats to Marine Resources

## KEY CONCEPTS

**1** Nets and Bycatch

**2** Land Runoff

**3** Pollution at Sea

**4** Damage to Coral Reefs

**5** Noise Pollution

Shrimp fishing drags a heavy trawl across the bottom of the sea. It collects unwanted animals and damages the seafloor habitat. Today's marine resources are at risk in many ways. Most of the threats come from humans and their way of life. People are more aware of some threats than they are of others.

## 1 Nets and Bycatch

In the 1980s, thousands of miles (km) of drift nets captured creatures in the world's oceans and seas. Drift netting produced enormous catches. It also produced huge numbers of bycatch. Bycatch are animals that are not commercially valuable. This includes animals that are too small, are damaged, or are not good to eat or popular as a food source. About 20 percent of catches on commercial fishing vessels are thrown back into the water.

Bycatch includes huge numbers of dolphins, whales, sharks, and other marine animals. These animals often get caught and drown. Seabirds also get caught in the nets. Recent studies in the Baltic Sea reported that 90,000 seabirds died from drift nets each year.

Drift nets are often lost or abandoned at sea because of storms, strong currents, accidents, or other factors. Called "ghost nets," they continue drifting, trapping ocean creatures, and causing great damage to the ocean environment. An international agreement now restricts the length of drifting gill nets to 1.6 miles (2.5 km).

As much as 90 percent of a shrimp trawl may be bycatch.

# 2 Land Runoff

Pollution that comes from land, such as **runoff** from farmland, affects the world's oceans. Rainwater carries nitrogen from the soil into streams and rivers that flow into the ocean. There, the nitrogen contributes to algal blooms that kill marine life.

Since the 1960s, the use by farmers of chemical fertilizers containing nitrogen has increased nine times. An additional increase of 50 percent is expected over the next 40 years to feed a growing world population. A 2013 UN report called for a major global review of the environmental damage caused by nitrogen fertilizers. The report called for nations to enact laws limiting their use.

Runoff containing **pesticides** sprayed on crops also endangers fish and other marine life. These chemicals cause diseases that harm fish populations. If industrial waste is dumped into rivers and oceans, metals such as mercury may harm not only fish but humans who eat fish containing mercury.

Septic tanks and cars release waste into the ground. Some of this waste washes into the sea. Particles put into the air from coal-burning power plants and other sources fall to the ground in rainwater. These particles add to the pollution flowing into the sea.

Correcting the damage caused by land runoff is costly. Each year, nations spend millions of dollars to restore and protect areas damaged or endangered by runoff pollution. This includes coastal fisheries.

The motor vehicles of drivers around the world are constantly dropping small amounts of oil each day onto roads and parking lots. This increases damaging runoff.

# Should the Use of Chemical Fertilizers Be Limited More?

**W**hile fertilizer use has made it possible for farms to produce more food, it has also had harmful effects on the land and on the sea. Experts have questioned the widespread use of chemical fertilizers. Limiting or banning chemical fertilizers would benefit fishers. However, it could result in fields that produce fewer crops and a decrease in income for farmers.

### Fishers

Chemical fertilizers may help farmers, but they do not help the fish population. In order for the fishing industry to survive, chemical fertilizers must be limited or banned altogether. I need to make a living just like everyone else. It is not fair for workers in the fishing industry to pay the price alone.

### Environmentalists

The use of chemical fertilizers should be cut back severely. Far too much is used in certain situations and locations, causing many types of damage to the environment.

### UN Scientists

It is unfortunate that fertilizers result in some environmental damage. However, there are benefits to farms producing more food. Fertilizer use needs to be managed globally.

### Farmers

Chemical fertilizer use is already limited. If there are any more limits on these fertilizers, I cannot earn what I need to operate my farm and support my family. Not enough food will be grown to feed the world's people.

| For | Supportive | Undecided | Unsupportive | Against |

# 3 Pollution at Sea

Ships themselves pollute the ocean waters. Tankers and offshore oil platforms can leak dangerous materials that damage sea life. When larger spills occur, clean up can take years. The long-term effects on the ecosystem are still unclear. Despite laws against dumping, many ships still release their sewage, or liquid and solid waste, into the seawater. Container ships, are cargo vessels that carry goods in large metal containers stacked on the ship's deck. Especially during storms, containers may slide off the deck into the sea. Experts say that more than 10,000 containers are lost each year. Over time, the containers decay and release their contents into the water. This often causes pollution.

Plastics pose another ocean pollution problem. Bottles, containers, and other plastic litter can choke or strangle marine life. Plastic material and other waste can become concentrated in areas with large circular surface currents called gyres. The North Pacific Gyre, also known as the Great Pacific Garbage Patch, takes up an area twice the size of Texas.

Ballast discharges have affected sea life. Ballast is heavy material, such as seawater, that a ship takes on to balance its weight. Ships often discharge their ballast after unloading their cargo when they reach port. Ballast water, however, may bring unwanted sea animals from one part of the world to another. For example, a type of jellyfish transported in a ship's ballast water was responsible for wiping out a number of food fish populations in the Black Sea in the 1980s and 1990s.

The UN Environment Program has estimated that every square mile (2.6 sq. km) of ocean contains 46,000 pieces of floating plastic.

Healthy coral reefs contain thousands of species that live nowhere else on Earth.

## 4 Damage to Coral Reefs

Coral reefs cover less than one percent of the ocean floor. However, they support 25 percent of all marine creatures. Reefs are formed from the skeletons of corals, tiny marine animals, that build up over thousands of years. Some coral reefs are estimated to be 50 million years old.

Coral reefs are found in shallow waters in tropical regions near Earth's equator. A wide variety of species live among these reefs, including many sea creatures people rely on for food. Medicines are also developed from the animals and plants that live in the reefs. The value of coral reefs has been estimated at $375 billion a year.

Coral reefs around the world are in danger. According to scientists, overfishing, sewage, runoff, and increased sea temperatures caused by **climate change** have put 70 percent of the world's coral reefs at risk of destruction. Overfishing causes an imbalance in a reef's ecosystem, leading to the death of the corals. Sewage and runoff poison the creatures that make the reef home. High water temperatures cause the tiny plants the corals eat to die, killing the corals themselves.

The number of corals in the Indian Ocean has dropped by 20 percent, and 80 percent of the remaining corals are at risk. About 70 percent of the corals around the Philippines have died. Several nations, including Australia and the United States, have declared Marine Protected Areas, or MPAs, around coral reefs to help safeguard them from pollution and other threats.

# 5 Noise Pollution

A recent threat to ocean life is noise pollution. With growing human activity on the oceans comes more and louder sounds. The three most important sources of ocean noise pollution are ship noise, oil and gas exploration, and military sonar.

When it is moving, an oil tanker generates underwater noise that is similar to a commercial jet taking off.

Large cargo vessels, the supertankers that transport oil, and cruise ships are in constant motion across the waters. Their engines, propellers, and other equipment make noises that spread beneath the waves. The oil and gas industry uses extremely loud noises to help determine the location of oil deposits below the ocean floor. Blasted every 10 to 60 seconds for days or months at a time, the noises disturb whales and other ocean life. Offshore platforms that drill for oil also generate loud noises. In order to detect underwater craft over long distances, military sonar systems send out powerful underwater noises.

Sound carries five times faster in water than in air. That is because water is more dense than air, and sound waves are transferred more quickly and efficiently. Through the ages, fish and other animals have learned to take advantage of all the natural underwater sea sounds. For marine life, hearing is the main sense. Sea mammals, such as dolphins and whales, use sound for navigation and communication. Fish, too, are sensitive to sound.

There is not enough evidence, say scientists, to determine the full amount of harm done to sea life by noise pollution. Some scientists believe that the noise works to confuse marine life. That affects their feeding, breeding, and other activities.

# Should Underwater Sonar Testing Be Stopped?

**M**ilitary sonar systems were first developed by the U.S. Navy to find enemy submarines. The regular testing of the latest technology seems to disrupt the pattern of marine life, especially dolphins and whales, who use sound to communicate. Environmentalists have asked the U.S. Navy to stop the testing. However, it continues to occur.

**Environmentalists**
Sonar testing must be stopped. It is harming sea life. It may already have caused the death of some whales and dolphins. There is nothing more important than protecting the oceans and their animals.

**Ocean Scientists**
We are still studying the effects of human produced sounds on sea life. Until we gather conclusive proof, it would be best to stop sonar testing. Everyone agrees that national security is a priority, but we need to limit testing, at least during times of peace.

**U.S. Citizens**
On one side, it would be shame to harm animal life. However, our national security is more important. No one wants our national security put at risk to save a few dolphins.

**U.S. Naval Officers**
Underwater sonar testing is absolutely crucial to our national defense. Until we have conclusive proof that it harms sea life, we must continue testing.

For          Supportive          Undecided          Unsupportive          Against

# The Future of Fishing

## KEY CONCEPTS

**1** Sustainable Development

**2** Genetically Engineered Fish

**3** Climate Change

T oday's world population is more than 7 billion. It is expected to reach 9.6 billion by the year 2050. Some experts question whether fishers will be able to catch or raise enough fish to feed an expanding population. Answers may lie in using science to breed new kinds of fish and raising larger amounts of fish in aquaculture. However, climate change may pose significant problems for the future of fishing.

## 1 Sustainable Development

Developing sustainable fisheries around the world is a major challenge. Working to end illegal fishing and establishing catch quotas based on fish populations are important first steps. However, the world's nations must also address a range of environmental issues.

## World Capture of Fish and Shellfish by Country

In 2011, the world capture of fish and shellfish totaled 103,059,000 tons (93,494,000 tonnes).

1. China 17,386 (15,772)
2. Peru 9,092 (8,248)
3. Indonesia 6,292 (5,708)
4. United States 5,680 (5,153)
5. India 4,742 (4,302)
6. Russia 4,690 (4,255)
7. Japan 4,146 (3,761)
8. Myanmar 3,674 (3,333)
9. Chile 3,376 (3,063)
10. Vietnam 2,759 (2,503)
All Other Countries 41,222 (37,396)

```
0    10,000   20,000   30,000   40,000
     (9,000)  (18,000) (27,000) (36,000)
```
**Thousands of Tons (Tonnes)**

## 2 Genetically Engineered Fish

The future of the seafood industry may be **genetic engineering**. While genetically modified (GM) crops have been raised for years, GM fish have not. Scientists in Massachusetts have created a genetically modified Atlantic salmon. It has two genes from other species of salmon to make it grow faster. It also has an added gene from an eel to make it grow all year long. The U.S. Food and Drug Administration is in the process of deciding whether to allow such GM salmon to be sold as a food fish in the United States.

Some scientists think this is just the beginning. Widespread development of GM fish, they believe, could have a major impact on the future supply of food fish. Genetic engineering could eventually develop many types of larger, more nutritious fish. It could produce fish that are more resistant to disease. It could result in fish that taste better. GM fish might also be a major new source of protein for an increasing world population, especially in developing countries.

## 3 Climate Change

A major unknown factor for the future of world fishing is climate change. The word climate describes the typical weather conditions for a large area of the planet over a long period of time. Many scientists who believe that climate change is now occurring predict that its effects may include melting ice caps in polar regions, rising sea levels, and more powerful storms. These scientists think that climate change will have significant effects on Earth's food supply, including fishing.

Despite scientific and technological advances, fishing today still depends on patterns of ocean currents. These currents, which move ocean water from one part of the world to another, help determine the water temperature in different regions. Some types of fish, known as cold-water fish, need cold water to survive. Warm-water fish thrive in warmer water. Some scientists believe that climate change could alter ocean currents and water temperatures in many areas. As a result, fish could die by the billions. Major sources of food could disappear.

If such predictions are correct, a major challenge ahead for the fishing industry and world governments may be dealing with climate change as it takes place. A number of scientists believe that human activities, such as burning coal and oil that adds carbon dioxide to the air, are a major cause of climate change. These scientists believe that people should be making changes in their way of life now that might avoid or slow down climate change for the future.

Some experts say climate change will produce more hurricanes and other severe storms on land and sea.

# Should People Be Concerned about Climate Change?

To many scientists and environmentalists, climate change is a major cause of concern. They believe a rise in global temperatures may bring with it crises on land and in the sea. Others believe that climate change happens so slowly that it will not have a major effect on human and animal life. Some people favor taking steps to try to prevent climate change. Others question whether there is anything that people can do. They think that changes in climate tend to occur naturally during Earth's history and are not related to human activities.

**Climate Scientists**
Mounting evidence suggests that Earth's climate is undergoing important changes and that people's use of certain fuels is a major cause. The whole planet is likely to be affected in dramatic ways if we don't take action now to try to reverse the trend.

**Oceanographers**
Climate change is already having an impact on marine ecosystems. If left unchecked, climate change may lead to the loss of entire species of food fish.

**Some Government Officials**
Climate change might be an issue of some concern. However, we have other more important issues we must worry about first, such as job growth and government debt.

**Some Citizens**
It is pointless to worry about something that we think is beyond our control. In any case, climate change probably will not affect our lives in any significant way.

For          Supportive          Undecided          Unsupportive          Against

# Fishing through History

Fishing has changed dramatically in the past 40,000 years. It is likely to continue changing.

**About 40,000 BC**

## About 40,000 BC

People living near seacoasts around the world use spears, hooks, and nets to catch fish.

## 800 BC

A Chinese writer first describes fish farming, or aquaculture.

## 110 BC

The Romans gather oysters from the water.

## AD 1300

Selling Baltic Sea herring preserved with salt is a major industry.

## 1376

English fishers invent the trawl net.

## 1497

Italian explorer John Cabot discovers cod stocks off the coast of Labrador.

## 1611

In England, the first ship built for hunting whales is completed.

## 1864

In Colorado, the first factory for canning salmon is established.

**1497**

## 1871

The U.S. Commission of Fish and Fisheries, now the National Marine Fisheries Service, is created.

## 1878

As stocks are depleted, cod catches in the North Atlantic Ocean decline sharply.

## 1902

The International Council for the Exploration of the Sea (ICES) is created to promote cooperation in ocean and fisheries science.

## 1903

Canned albacore tuna is available to consumers.

1903

## 1960

The global fish catch is 40 million tons (36 million tonnes), twice the amount caught in 1950.

2014

## 1972

Iceland becomes the first country to claim an extended fishing zone of 50 nautical miles (90 km) from its coasts.

## 1976

Congress passes the Magnuson-Stevens Act to manage fisheries in waters controlled by the United States.

## 1982

The UN Convention on the Law of the Sea (UNCLOS) establishes exclusive economic zones up to 200 nautical miles (370 km) from official coastlines.

## 1992

Canada declares a freeze on cod fishing after a sudden decline in stocks.

## 1994

UNCLOS officially has binding force.

## 2011

Five tuna species are officially categorized as **threatened** in the United States.

## 2014

An FAO report predicts fish farms will produce almost two-thirds of the world's fish supply by 2030.

# Fishing Careers

## FISHER

**Duties**  Fishing at sea

**Education**  A high school diploma

**Interest**  Working outdoors and in a boat for long periods of time

Fishers usually begin their careers as deckhands and receive on-the-job training. They often find their jobs through family members. Companies that run large trawlers and fish-processing ships accept applications through human resources departments. An experienced fisher may become first mate, which is an assistant to the captain, then a boatswain, who supervises the deckhands, and eventually captain.

## MARINE BIOLOGIST

**Duties**  Studying marine organisms and their habitats

**Education**  A university degree in science, with biology as a major area of study

**Interest**  Working in the ocean and protecting the environment

Marine biologists should enjoy being in and near the water. Their work may involve wading through mucky swamps, snorkeling or deep-sea diving, traveling in small motorboats to collect water samples, or spending weeks aboard large research vessels. Marine biologists must understand the **biochemistry** of aquatic organisms. Some marine biologists study animals that are used for food. Others study the effects of natural and human-related disasters, such as oil spills, on the marine environment.

## FISH FARMER

**Duties**  Raise fish on land and in the sea

**Education**  A high school diploma or college degree

**Interest**  Working outdoors and studying marine science

Fish farmers work as part of a team that is responsible for breeding and raising fish and shellfish, monitoring water conditions, harvesting stock, and selling the products. Responsibilities include hatching eggs from adult stock, purchasing young fish, and monitoring the health of the stock. Fish farm managers have to maintain the farm's equipment and check water temperature and oxygen content. Aquaculture requires excellent problem solving skills. People often need to work long hours, and fish farmers must be physically fit.

## OCEANOGRAPHER

**Duties**  Study the oceans and their connections to other environments

**Education**  A college degree, with math or engineering as a major area of study

**Interest**  Understanding complex environmental interactions, problem solving, and working outdoors

Oceanographers collect and study data related to the oceans, as well as other parts of the biosphere. They study tides, currents, marine life, and the atmosphere using field observations, computer models, and laboratory experiments. Oceanographers may work in universities, government agencies, environmental organizations, and various industries. A career in oceanography demands long periods of time spent away from home.

# Key Fishing Organizations

## FAO

**Goal**  Lead international efforts to defeat hunger

**Reach**  Worldwide

**Facts**  An agency of the United Nations that was founded in 1945

**The Food and Agriculture Organization of the UN (FAO)** is one of the largest agencies of the United Nations. It is the major agency dealing with issues involving agriculture, fisheries, forestry, and rural development. An intergovernmental organization, it has 183 member countries and a budget of $650 million per year. The FAO carries out hundreds of projects all over the world. Since the early 1960s, FAO efforts have helped reduced the proportion of hungry people in developing countries from more than 50 percent to less than 20 percent. The organization also encourages sustainable agriculture and rural development.

## GREENPEACE

**Goal**  Ensure the ability of Earth to support life in all its diversity

**Reach**  Worldwide

**Facts**  A nongovernmental environmental organization that focuses on climate change, deforestation, commercial whaling, and overfishing

**Greenpeace** grew out of antinuclear protests in the late 1960s and 1970s. In just a few years, the organization spread to several countries and began to campaign about world environmental issues. Greenpeace is known for taking direct action on the sea, such as confronting illegal whaling vessels. The organization does not accept funding from governments, corporations, or political parties. It relies on grants from nonprofit groups and contributions from 2.9 million individual supporters.

## MSC

**Goal** Promote sustainable fisheries

**Reach** Worldwide

**Facts** An independent nonprofit organization

**The Marine Stewardship Council (MSC)** is made up of independent experts who recommend standards for ocean fisheries. Seafood products that come from a sustainable source confirmed by the organization may display a blue MSC label. The MSC's mission is to use its label and fishery certification program to support the health of the world's oceans. The organization hopes to influence the choices people make when buying seafood to promote sustainable fisheries.

## IWC

**Goal** To regulate world whaling practices

**Reach** Worldwide

**Facts** An independent international body

**The International Whaling Commission (IWC)**, established by the International Convention for the Regulation of Whaling in 1946, encourages, coordinates, and funds whale research. It also publishes the results of scientific research and promotes whale and whaling studies. The main goal of the IWC is to review and revise, when needed, laws regulating the conduct of whaling throughout the world. The IWC has set limits on whale hunting areas and seasons, as well as barred the capture of young calves and female whales accompanied by calves. In some cases, it has provided for the complete protection of certain whale species.

# Research a Fishing Issue

## The Issue

Fishing regulation is a subject of much debate. Many groups may not agree on the best way to maintain fish stocks, help fishers, or feed the world's people. It is important to enter into a discussion to hear all the points of view before making decisions. Discussing issues will make sure that the actions taken are beneficial for all involved.

## Get the Facts

Choose an issue (political, cultural, economic, or ecological) from this book. Then, pick one of the four groups presented in the issue spectrum. Using the book and research in the library or on the Internet, find out more about the group you chose. What is important to members of this group? Why are they backing or opposing the particular issue? What claims or facts can they use to support their point of view? Be sure to write clear and concise supporting arguments for your group. Focus on fishing regulation and the way the group's needs relate to it. Will this group be affected in a positive or negative way by action taken related to regulation?

## Use the Concept Web

A concept web can be a useful research tool. Read the information and review the structure in the concept web on the next page. Use the relationships between concepts to help you understand your group's point of view.

## Organize Your Research

Sort your information into organized points. Make sure your research answers clearly the impact the issue will have on your chosen group, how that impact will affect the group, and why the group has chosen its specific point of view.

# FISHING CONCEPT WEB

Use this concept web to understand the network of factors relating to world fishing.

- Pesticides and chemical fertilizers, which eventually wash into the sea, pollute the water.
- Ships pollute the water through oil spills and waste dumping.
- Large vessels moving on the ocean are one source of noise pollution.
- Today's global fishing methods damage the world's coral reefs.

- Quotas help safeguard a country's fishing resources.
- Strict enforcement of conservation laws helps protect fish stocks.

- Water temperatures affect the size of fish stocks.
- Climate change could affect the health of fish species.

Threats to Marine Resources

Climate Change

International Laws

WORLD FISHING

Large Industry

Seafood Consumption

Aquaculture

- Huge factory ships capture and process more seafood than ever before.
- Today's fishing businesses use many kinds of technology, including satellites.
- The bycatch created by the fishing industry damages animal life.

- Today's annual fish consumption is almost 37 pounds (17 kg) per person.
- Seafood is a healthy food choice for people in developed countries.
- Many developing countries rely on fish for protein.

- Fish farming is overtaking traditional fisheries.
- Nearly two-thirds of global aquaculture takes place in China.
- Genetically engineered fish crops might be a new food source.

# Test Your Knowledge

Answer each of the questions below to test your knowledge about world fishing.

**1** What percentage of Earth is covered by water?

**2** What is the name of the process by which ocean plants convert the Sun's energy into food?

**3** What is aquaculture?

**4** What does fish contain that may protect against heart disease and improve brain function?

**5** What continent has the highest consumption of seafood per person?

**6** What international agreement affecting fishing in areas near coastlines was adopted in 1982?

**7** What is a giant circular oceanic surface current called?

**8** What are coral reefs composed of?

**9** How much faster does sound travel in water than in air?

**10** Which country has nearly two-thirds of the world's fish farms?

**ANSWERS 1.** 70 percent **2.** Photosynthesis **3.** Fish farming **4.** Omega-3 fatty acids **5.** Asia **6.** UN Convention on the Law of the Sea (UNCLOS) **7.** Gyre **8.** The skeletons of tiny marine animals **9.** Five times faster **10.** China

# Key Words

**algal blooms**: population explosions of algae that use up oxygen dissolved in water as they decay, so that aquatic animals suffocate

**barbs**: sharp points that stick out backward, as on a fishhook

**biochemistry**: chemistry that deals with the chemical compounds and processes occurring in organisms

**biodegradable**: capable of being broken down by the action of living things

**biosphere**: the parts of Earth and its atmosphere in which living things are found

**buoys**: objects that float on the water's surface, to mark a location or hold something in place

**climate change**: a change in Earth's average temperatures and other weather conditions over a long period of time, such as the major warming trend that most scientists agree has been taking place over the past century

**commercial**: related to earning money

**crustaceans**: hard-shelled animals, such as lobsters and shrimp, that live mostly in water and have jointed bodies

**developed countries**: countries with high average income and advanced technology

**developing countries**: countries with low average income that until recently had little manufacturing and technology

**distant-water ships**: fishing boats built to travel long distances and stay at sea for long periods of time

**endangered**: at risk of extinction

**extinction**: the complete dying off of a type of animals or plants, so that it no longer exist on Earth

**fishmeal**: ground dried fish used as fertilizer or animal feed

**genetic engineering**: the deliberate modification of the characteristics of an organism by changing its genes, which control its growth, appearance, and functioning

**gills**: the respiratory organs by which fish extract oxygen from water

**groundwater**: supplies of fresh water located below the ground

**harpoons**: spears used to catch large sea animals

**mollusks**: soft-bodied animals, such as clams, that have no backbones and usually live in salt water

**organisms**: forms of life

**pesticides**: chemicals used to kill harmful pests

**photosynthesis**: the process used by plants to convert energy from sunlight into food

**protein**: a group of substances that are needed to make cell parts and to assist them in functioning

**retailers**: workers who sell a product to the people who will be using it

**runoff**: water that flows over an area of land into a body of water

**schools**: large numbers of fish belonging to the same species that are swimming together

**species**: a group of individuals with common characteristics

**stock**: the number of fish in a certain area

**sustainable**: capable of being maintained without harming the environment

**target fish**: the type of fish that a fishing boat is trying to catch

**threatened**: at risk of being endangered

**traditional fisheries**: a way of fishing that has been passed through generations

# Index

aquaculture 16, 33, 36
Asia 15
Atlantic Ocean 15, 37
Australia 29

ballast 28
biodiversity 7
bycatch 25

Canada 37
chemical fertilizers 26, 27
China 15, 16
climate change 29, 33, 34, 35, 40
cod 7, 15, 19, 36, 39
conservation 22
coral reefs 29
crabs 15

distant-water ships 19
dolphins 13, 25, 30, 31
drift nets 9, 25

ecosystem 7, 19, 28, 29, 35

factory ships 12
fishmeal 4, 12, 16, 18
Food and Agriculture Organization 18, 20, 37, 40

garum 8
genetically engineered fish 33
gill nets 13, 25
Great Pacific Garbage Patch 28
Greenpeace 40
gyres 28

Iceland 22, 37
Indian Ocean 29
International Whaling Commission 41
Inuit people 18

Japan 18

longlining 9

marine biologist 38
Marine Stewardship Council 41

Nile River 8
noise pollution 30
North America 8, 10, 11

oceanographer 39
omega-3 fatty acids 18
overfishing 19, 29, 40
oysters 8, 16, 36

Pacific Ocean 12, 19, 20, 28
phytoplankton 7
purse nets 9

quotas 19, 22, 33

Russia 19

salmon 16, 33, 36
satellites 10
seals 19
shellfish 16, 39
shrimp 15, 16
sustainable development 33, 40, 41

traditional fisheries 10, 11, 12, 16
trawlers 9, 12, 38
trawl nets 9, 26, 36
tuna 7, 15, 17, 37

United Nations 18, 40
United Nations Convention on the Law
  of the Sea 22, 23, 37

whales 7, 13, 19, 25, 30, 31, 36, 41

# Log on to www.av2books.com

AV² by Weigl brings you media enhanced books that support active learning. Go to www.av2books.com, and enter the special code found on page 2 of this book. You will gain access to enriched and enhanced content that supplements and complements this book. Content includes video, audio, weblinks, quizzes, a slide show, and activities.

## AV² Online Navigation

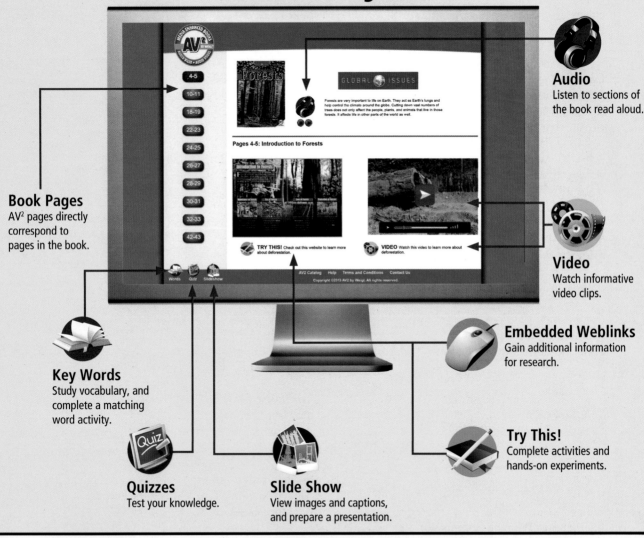

**Book Pages**
AV² pages directly correspond to pages in the book.

**Audio**
Listen to sections of the book read aloud.

**Video**
Watch informative video clips.

**Embedded Weblinks**
Gain additional information for research.

**Try This!**
Complete activities and hands-on experiments.

**Key Words**
Study vocabulary, and complete a matching word activity.

**Quizzes**
Test your knowledge.

**Slide Show**
View images and captions, and prepare a presentation.

AV² was built to bridge the gap between print and digital. We encourage you to tell us what you like and what you want to see in the future.

## Sign up to be an AV² Ambassador at www.av2books.com/ambassador.

Due to the dynamic nature of the Internet, some of the URLs and activities provided as part of AV² by Weigl may have changed or ceased to exist. AV² by Weigl accepts no responsibility for any such changes. All media enhanced books are regularly monitored to update addresses and sites in a timely manner. Contact AV² by Weigl at 1-866-649-3445 or av2books@weigl.com with any questions, comments, or feedback.